915.38   Fazio, Wende.
FAZ
          Saudi Arabia.

c. 78

                    34880030035278

$25.00

DATE			

SAUDI ARABIA

A TRUE BOOK

by
Wende Fazio

Children's Press®
A Division of Grolier Publishing
New York London Hong Kong Sydney
Danbury, Connecticut

Reading Consultant
Linda Cornwell
Learning Resource Consultant
Indiana Department of
Education

A young
Saudi boy

Visit Children's Press® on the
Internet at:
http://publishing.grolier.com

Library of Congress Cataloging-in-Publication Data

Fazio, Wende.
    Saudi Arabia / by Wende M. Fazio.
       p.   cm. — (A true book)
    Includes bibliographical references and index.
    Summary: Provides an overview of the geography, history, and culture
of the kingdom of Saudi Arabia.
    ISBN 0-516-21190-0 (lib. bdg.)   0-516-26502-4 (pbk.)
    1. Saudi Arabia—Juvenile literature. [1. Saudi Arabia.] I. Title.
II. Series.
DS204.F39   1999
915.38—dc21   98-12273
                                                                CIP
                                                                AC

GROLIER
PUBLISHING

Contents

The Land and the Climate

The Kingdom of Saudi Arabia occupies four-fifths of the Arabian Peninsula with a population of more than 20 million people. The land is divided into four major geographical regions: the Najd, or central plateau, is in central Arabia; the Hejaz borders the Red Sea;

Asir lies along the Red Sea between the Hejaz and Yemen; and the Eastern Province known as Hasa lies along the Persian Gulf.

The land area of Saudi Arabia is about 830,000 square miles (2,149,690 square kilometers). The peninsula has two mountain regions: the Hejaz region in the north, and the Asir region in the south. The Hejaz separates the desert from the coastal plain.

The Asir region receives up to 12 inches (30 cm) of rainfall a year.

The Asir is one of the few regions of Saudi Arabia that gets some rainfall. It is often called "the garden of Saudi Arabia" because it is so green and fertile.

Southern Saudi Arabia has a harsh, windswept desert called the Rub-Al-Khali, or the Empty Quarter.

The Empty Quarter is the largest sand desert in the world, covering more than 250,000 square miles (650,000 sq km). Its landscape is always changing as strong winds and sandstorms move its massive dunes. Some of these dunes are more than 1,000 feet (300 meters) high. The An-Nafûd

The Empty Quarter is the largest body of sand in the world.

Desert lies north of the Empty Quarter. During the summer, the deserts have daytime temperatures as high as 130°F (54° Celsius).

Najd means "heartland" in central Arabia.

Between these two great deserts is the region known as the Najd, or the heartland of

Saudi Arabia. Most of the land in this region is rocky with dry riverbed valleys and oases. The capital of Saudi Arabia, Riyadh, is located here.

East of the Najd is the Hasa, or Eastern Provinces. This region is made up of sand and gravel plains, with salt flats along the coastline. The Hasa has the world's largest deposits of oil, the source of Saudi Arabia's vast wealth.

Black Gold: Oil

The first oil well site in Saudi Arabia

The development of the oil industry has changed Saudi Arabia. Oil made a very poor country into a land of great wealth.

Petroleum, or crude oil, is a thick, dark liquid that will burn and produce energy. When crude oil is refined, it is changed into other products that are used every day, such as gasoline to power cars, lawnmowers, and even small airplanes.

Holding tanks store the oil.

Crude oil can also be refined to produce petrochemicals.

Petrochemicals are used to make plastic, artificial rubber, fibers for clothing, dyes, cosmetics, paint, ink, and even medicines.

This oil plant provides motor gas and jet fuel to countries throughout the world.

The History of Saudi Arabia

Until 1932, Saudi Arabia was called Arabia. Long ago, traders crossed Arabia on caravan routes into Egypt and other Middle Eastern countries. Trading centers along the caravan routes supplied pack animals, food, and lodging for the traders. One of these cities was Mecca.

14

In the 1800s, most traders traveled in caravans.

Mecca is the birthplace of the prophet Muhammad and the religion of Islam. Even before Muhammad's birth in A.D. 570, Mecca was a holy city. Religious travelers, called

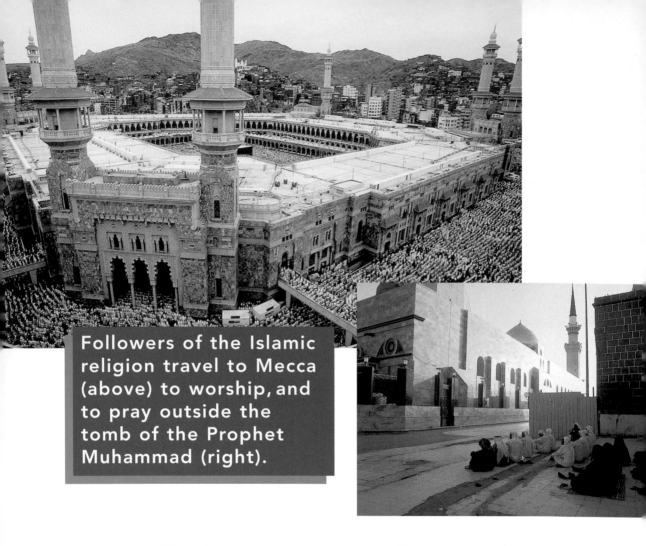

Followers of the Islamic religion travel to Mecca (above) to worship, and to pray outside the tomb of the Prophet Muhammad (right).

pilgrims, came to Mecca to worship many gods. When Muhammad was 35 years old, he began to tell the people

16

about his visions. He said God had chosen him to tell people to start worshiping the one and only God called Allah.

Muhammad made enemies because many people did not want to stop worshiping their pagan gods. His enemies made him leave Mecca, but this did not stop Muhammad. Soon his teachings spread over much of Arabia.

When Islam spread throughout Arabia, most of

the land was still ruled by
nomads—people who wan-
dered from one place to
another, feeding their animals.
Nomads lived together in
groups called clans or tribes,
and different tribes would
often fight each other.

Modern Saudi Arabia began
in 1902, when Abdul-Aziz ibn
Saud became head of the
Saud clan. Ibn Saud wanted to
unite all the tribes and clans of
Arabia into one society under
Islamic law. Ibn Saud had to

fight many battles to unite Arabia, but finally, in 1925, he won the last great desert battle. Arabia became the Kingdom of Saudi Arabia in September 1932, with Ibn Saud as its king. Today, Saudi Arabia is still governed by the Saud family. King Fahd has ruled since 1982.

King Fahd succeeded the throne following the death of his half brother, King Khalid.

The Religion of Islam

Islam has always been important in this region, even before Saudi Arabia became a kingdom. For the followers of Islam, who are called Muslims, religion governs every part of life.

Five duties are expected of all Muslims: declaring their faith, praying five times daily,

Honoring the duties of their Islamic religion, these students take time out to pray.

giving to the poor, fasting, and making at least one pilgrimage to Mecca. Parts of the Koran, the holy book of Islam, are similar to the Christian Bible.

Muhammad's message to the people of Mecca centered on the belief in one God, called "Allāh."

Muslims believe that the Koran records the word of God as spoken to Muhammad. The Koran also serves as Saudi Arabia's constitution, creating a system of laws for the people and the government to live by.

Town and Desert People

Deep in the deserts of Saudi Arabia, nomads live in tents made of goat hair. These nomads are called the Bedouin. *Bedouin* comes from an Arabic word meaning "camel-herder in the desert."

The Bedouin move constantly in search of water and

Approximately one-third of Saudi Arabia's people are nomads.

grazing lands for their camels, sheep, and goats. Their way of life has not changed for thousands of years.

Most Saudi Arabians live and work in cities. Many homes in the cities are built around a central courtyard. The court-

Courtyard walls keep this family safe from desert winds.

yard walls provide shade from the sun and protection from the high winds that blow in from the desert. Often, several generations of families live in the same house or join their houses by building walled-in compounds.

Saudi men wear a long, flowing white robe called a *thobe* that covers them from neck to feet. A cotton *ghutra* is worn on their head, and held in place by a black cord

These Saudi men, dressed in their thobe and ghutra, enjoy a cup of coffee, another Saudi tradition.

Two young Saudi girls wear their abayas as they walk to school.

called an *agal*. The thobe and ghutra protect them from the fierce sun and desert heat.

Most Saudi women cover their face with a veil when in public, and wear a floor-length black robe called an *abaya*. They wear colorful, traditional dresses under the abaya. Elderly women dress from head to toe in black. Children like Western-style clothing, but they wear uniforms to school.

Plants and Animals of Saudi Arabia

Trees and plants are a rare sight in Saudi Arabia because of the lack of rain and the poor soil. The mountain region of Asir has the only forest in Saudi Arabia. Wild olive and juniper trees grow there. Fruit trees such as the fig, carob,

A Bedouin camel herder (left)
and the annual camel race (above)
held in honor of the king

and date palm also grow in the
mountains.

The desert climate is hard
on animal life, but some
species have adapted to the
harsh weather. Today, however,
the Bedouin use few camels
for transportation. Camels are

primarily kept for their meat and for the camel races held every spring. Sheep also provide meat, and goats are kept for goat cheese. The famous Arabian horse is bred for its beauty and endurance.

Meat-eaters such as wolves, hyenas, and jackals are common. Wild goats, called ibex, and baboons live in the mountain regions.

Snakes, lizards, scorpions, and locusts, or grasshoppers,

The Arabian horse (left) and the ibex (above) are two of the many animals found in Saudi Arabia.

are all found in Saudi Arabia. The scorpion and snakes such as vipers and cobras are very poisonous.

The Camel

The camel is a hardy animal, well-adapted to desert life. Camels can go for days, and even weeks, without water.

The camel, or dromedary, has a single hump on its back, which stores fat. The camel has pads on its feet that help it to walk on sand. Its heavy eyelids and eyelashes protect its eyes against sun and blowing sand. Camels are sometimes called "ships of the desert."

Natural Resources

Saudi Arabia is rich in oil. Today, more and more oil fields are being discovered. Saudi Arabia is now the third-largest producer of oil in the world.

Saudi Arabia has other resources as well. Minerals such as gold, silver, lead, and copper are plentiful. Zinc, nickel, pyrite (used to produce sulfuric acid), phosphate, and gypsum (used to make plaster) are also important.

Although the discovery of oil transformed Saudi Arabia's economy, farming and raising livestock are still a way of life for rural people.

Wheat is Saudi Arabia's principal crop, along with rice, alfalfa, barley, and grapes. Cotton, melon, and other fruits are also grown.

Although the petroleum industry (top) dominates Saudi Arabia's economy, farming (left) and herding (below) have remained the traditional occupations of the people.

Saudi Arabia Today

For thousands of years, Saudi Arabia was a poor country. Then in 1938 oil was discovered there. Oil production began in 1945, bringing in large amounts of money.

Since then, many roads, schools, hospitals, and houses have been built. Bedouins

An aerial view of Riyadh, the country's capital city

have begun to settle in the cities, where they can earn good wages. Also, many foreigners have moved into the cities to work in the oil industry. Today,

A formal system of education was initiated during the 1930s.

more than 84 percent of the Saudi Arabian people live in cities.

English is taught throughout the country, but Arabic is the official language. The Arabic language uses a different alphabet from English. The written language uses flowing, rounded, and connected characters that are read from right to left.

Before Islam, poetry and stories were common forms of entertainment. These poems and stories celebrated love and heroes, but Muhammad did not approve, so poetry is no longer popular. Television and radio are popular sources of entertainment today.

Camel racing, horse racing, and hunting with dogs or

falcons are the favorite traditional sports of Saudi Arabia. Recently, basketball and soccer have become popular.

Saudi Arabia's government continues to be a monarchy, ruled by the Saud family. The king is the head of state and of the government. The power of the king is based on Islamic law.

Saudi Arabia has seen many changes during its history, but strong love of family

These Saudi families enjoy time together, in accordance with the Islamic religion.

and the faith of Islam are still the most important values in Saudi Arabia today.

To Find Out More

Here are more places to learn about Saudi Arabia:

Books

The Arabian Peninsula.
George Constable, ed.
Time-Life Books, 1985.

Arnold, Caroline. **Camel.**
Morrow, 1992.

King, John. **Bedouin.**
RaintreeSteck-Vaughn,
1992.

Petersen, David. **Asia.**
Children's Press, 1998.

Tames, Richard. **Muslim.**
Children's Press, 1996.

Organizations and Online Sites

General Culture Links, Saudi Arabia

http://saudi-online.com/ culture/general.html

From clothing to art, this website provides an indepth look at the culture of the Saudi Arabian people.

The Kingdom of Saudi Arabia Home Page

http://www.saudi.net

Provides video clips, audio clips, and general information about Saudi Arabia, plus current news and press releases.

The Royal Embassy of Saudi Arabia

http://www.saudicommercial office.com/

Information Office
601 New Hampshire Avenue, NW
Washington, D.C. 20037
All kinds of exciting information on the kingdom of Saudi Arabia, including links and addresses for additional research.

Saudi Arabia: Islam

http://imed.saudi.net/ profile/islam/islam-sa.html

This site provides an overview to the history of the Islamic religion, the prophet Muhammad, and the holy city of Mecca.

Important Words

caravan a group of people travelling together for safety

generation the average amount of time between the birth of parents and the birth of their children

idol an image that is usually worshipped as a god

Islam the religious faith of Muslims; an Arabic word for "submission" and "peace"

nomad a wanderer with no permanent home

oasis a place in the desert where water and plants grow

pagan a person who is not a member of a religious group and who does not believe in one specific God

Index

Meet the Author

Wende Fazio lives in Elizabeth, New Jersey, with her husband. She received her B.A. from Rutgers University, where she first was introduced to Middle Eastern romance literature and history. She is a freelance writer and has written several books on a variety of subjects. This is her third book for Children's Press.